Phonics
FUN
BOOK EIGHT

The HERD CAME in THIRD

Diphthongs and R-Controlled Vowels

3rd

Brian P. Cleary

Illustrations by **Jason Miskimins**

Consultant:
Alice M. Maday
PhD in Early Childhood Education with a Focus in Literacy
Assistant Professor, Retired
Department of Curriculum and Instruction
University of Minnesota

Lerner Publications ◆ Minneapolis

For Hazel

Lerner Publications Company
An imprint of Lerner Publishing Group, Inc.
241 First Avenue North
Minneapolis, MN 55401 USA

For reading levels and more information, look up this title at www.lernerbooks.com.

Main body text set in Mikado. Typeface provided by HVD.

Library of Congress Cataloging-in-Publication Data

Names: Cleary, Brian P., 1959- author. | Miskimins, Jason, illustrator. | Maday, Alice M., consultant.
Title: The herd came in third : diphthongs and r-controlled vowels / Brian P. Cleary ; illustrations by Jason Miskimins ; consultant: Alice M. Maday.
Description: Minneapolis : Lerner Publications, [2022] | Series: Phonics fun | Audience: Ages 4-8. | Audience: Grades 2-3. | Summary: "With rhyming, carefully leveled text and comedic, colorful illustrations, this book provides plenty of examples of diphthongs and r-controlled vowels and encourages readers to try the sounds for themselves"— Provided by publisher.
Identifiers: LCCN 2021033576 (print) | LCCN 2021033577 (ebook) | ISBN 9781728441320 (lib. bdg.) | ISBN 9781728448558 (pbk.) | ISBN 9781728444932 (eb pdf)
Subjects: LCSH: English language—Vowels—Juvenile literature. | English language—Consonants—Juvenile literature. | English language—Phonetics—Juvenile literature. | Reading—Phonetic method—Juvenile literature.
Classification: LCC PE1157 .C5473 2022 (print) | LCC PE1157 (ebook) | DDC 428.1/3—dc23

LC record available at https://lccn.loc.gov/2021033576
LC ebook record available at https://lccn.loc.gov/2021033577

Manufactured in the United States of America
3-53634-49746-7/7/2022

Dear Parents and Educators,

As a former adult literacy coach and the father of three children, I know that learning to read isn't always easy. That's why I developed **Phonics Fun**—a series that uses a combination of devices to help children learn to read. This book uses rhyme, repetition, illustration, and phonics to introduce young readers to diphthongs and R-controlled vowels. Words in bold all feature diphthongs and R-controlled vowels.

The bridge to literacy is one of the most important we will ever cross. It is my hope that the Phonics Fun series will help young readers to hop, gallop, and skip from one side to the other!

Sincerely,

Brian P. Cleary

Note to Readers

This book is all about diphthongs and R-controlled vowels. You can hear diphthongs and R-controlled vowels in words like **foil** and **shirt**. The **bold** words in this book have diphthongs and R-controlled vowels. They also rhyme!

He poured **oil** on the **foil** on the **soil**.

house

The **mouse** took the **blouse** from her **house.**

The **herd** and the **bird** came in **third**.

The girl with the **bow** will **mow** grass in a **row**.

row

The **cow** by the **plow** will eat her **chow now.**

plow

The **clown** in the **gown** has a **brown crown.**

Bert got **dirt** on her **skirt** and **shirt**.

The **scout** had to **shout** when he looked out and saw a **trout** with a **spout**.

Make Your Own

Use the words on these pages to write a story with diphthongs and R-controlled vowels!

oil

shirt

mouse

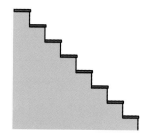

stairs

tar

snow

skirt

soil

chairs

blouse

crow

car

Poet, literacy enthusiast, and word nerd **Brian P. Cleary** "grew up" in one of the largest creative divisions in the world, where he has put words in the mouths of Dolly Parton, William Shatner, and Kevin Nealon. He has written many best-selling grammar and poetry books for young readers.

Jason Miskimins graduated from the Columbus College of Art & Design in 2003. He works as an illustrator of books and greeting cards.

Alice M. Maday has a master's degree in early childhood education from Butler University and a PhD in early childhood education, with a focus on literacy, from the University of Minnesota. Her research interests include kindergarten curriculum, emergent literacy, parent and teacher expectations, and the place of preschool in the reading readiness process.